AF483617

To my wife, Gabriele, who encouraged my big-as-an-elephant dreams of becoming a writer, and to my daughters Christine and Celine, that you may have a future with wild elephants in it.

-RGdeR

Mother To Elephants

The Story of Daphne Sheldrick

R.G. de Rouen

Illustrated by Kateryna Rohotova

Daphne doubted there was anything more beautiful than her home in Africa's Great Rift Valley.

She loved its openness, its sky of radiant blue, and most of all...
its animals.

Great herds dotted the landscape like spots on a leopard.
And she imagined herself among them.

Wild and free!

Walking with wild things was completely normal for Daphne.

There was Bob the impala, waterbuck Daisy, and mongoose Ricky-Ticky-Tavey. All were animals her parents cared for on their farm in Kenya.

What birdcall was that? Which creature had left its mark in the mud?

To Daphne, the wonder of nature was everywhere.

When Daphne was quite young, she was put in charge of an orphaned antelope. She named him Bushy and was determined to be the mother he had lost.

"A wild animal is only borrowed," her father reminded her,
"If you truly love it, you must set it free when nature calls."

Daphne promised. Yet, not wanting to lose Bushy, she hung a
little cowbell around his neck.

TING, TING, TING the bell sounded as he trotted
after her.

Until one day…

Bushy was gone. Daphne's tears could have flooded a river. She would
have given anything to have her little friend back.

Daphne grew up to marry a man who shared her love for animals and nature. David Sheldrick was the head warden of a large national park called Tsavo.

They would often camp by a waterhole and watch as the animals came to drink.

Their favorites were the elephants. Silently and gracefully they appeared. Joyful trumpeting and rumbling filled the air as the elephants greeted each other.

How majestic they were!

Daphne and David wished everyone felt the same way about these marvellous animals.

Unfortunately, not all did.

Poachers entered the park to hunt for elephant ivory. David sent rangers by air and ground to stop them.

Sadly, they often found little elephants that had lost their mothers due to these hunters.

It was Daphne who would care for them.

One day a truck arrived with the tiniest elephant.
Daphne's heart sank. She knew it needed its mother's milk.
Yet, no one had ever raised an elephant that young before.

Could Daphne?

Daphne tried mixing different milk formulas for the elephant she named Aisha. Cow milk. Baby formula. Nothing worked. Aisha was getting weaker by the day.

Then, one tin caught Daphne's eye. It contained coconut oil. Would this work?

It did!
Soon, Aisha got stronger and followed Daphne everywhere...

in the garden,

on nature walks,

and even for morning tea on the lawn.

That's when Daphne knew. This baby elephant had decided that she was her mother!

All was well for months until Daphne left home for a few days.
Aisha became heartsick and refused to drink her milk.

Daphne rushed back home, but it was too late!

Daphne cried bitterly as she realized her mistake. Aisha had grown too attached to her. Baby elephants living in the wild had an entire herd to guide and protect them.

Daphne was determined to give any new orphans just that.

She hired and trained keepers to help care for the orphaned elephants day and night.

Feeding time was special.

The keepers used a helpful trick to bottle feed the youngest. They hid behind huge blankets that felt like their elephant mother's warm body.

Of course, there was also playtime!

The elephants delighted in splashing and
pushing each other around in the mud,

blowing bubbles in their water troughs...

or kicking soccer balls with their keepers!

After a fun-filled day, not everyone was ready for bed.
Some elephants needed to be lured back into their pens with another
bottle of milk.

Covered with soft blankets, the elephants spent the night next to their caretakers. Keepers rotated every day, so that the elephants wouldn't depend on just one person, as Aisha had done with Daphne.

News of Daphne's Orphan Project soon grew like the trees she had planted around her home.

Daphne now had the ingredients to help baby elephants.
It was her special formula, and lots and lots of motherly love!

Over time, the elephants grew big enough to rejoin the wild herds.

Joy filled Daphne's heart! She remembered the words from her father so long ago that to truly love a wild animal in your care is to set it free.

She watched as dozens of her previous orphans came from many miles away to greet the newcomers.

Then, it was back to a new beginning.

A life wild and free!

Right Tusked Or Left Tusked?

Elephants use their tusks for many things like stripping bark off trees, digging, lifting, fighting off predators, or for battles with other elephants. But did you know that just as humans are right-handed or left-handed, elephants can be right-tusked or left-tusked? The preferred tusk is known as the master tusk.

Super Sunscreen!

You've now discovered that elephants enjoy a good mud bath. But splashing around in the wet mud is not just for fun. Just like children put on sunscreen to go swimming at the beach or pool, elephants need to do this too. It may not seem like it, but their thick skin is very sensitive. To protect from the hot sun, elephants will cake on mud or sand. This also acts to ward off pesky insects! Once dry, they have instant sunscreen.

Muscle Control

Elephant trunks are powerful enough to uproot a tree, but delicate enough to pick up even the tiniest berry. However, elephants are not born with the ability to control the thousands of muscles that are in their trunks. They have to learn this. Elephant babies are known to even stumble over their own trunks in the beginning. Imagine falling over your own nose!

Mighty Memory

With their amazing memories, elephants can find old forage pathways and locate water sources many miles away. Elephants can find water holes they haven't visited in years or recognize elephants they've met long ago. So, an elephant really does never forget!

My, What Big Ears You Have!

An elephant's ears are about 1/6 its body size and, besides being super hearing receptors, they are great at keeping an elephant cool. By merely flapping their ears like giant fans when no wind is present, elephants can make their body temperatures sink by 10 degrees Fahrenheit (12 degrees Celsius). When a wind is blowing, elephants will face into it and spread their ears to capture its coolness.

Hearing With Your Feet?

Over a short distance, elephants pick up sound, like we do, through their ears. Over a long distance, scientists have confirmed that elephants are able to hear through their feet. The sound waves caused by trumpeting become tremors that elephants in the distance can pick up with their feet. Talk about making a long-distance call!

Super Spreader

While elephants walk up to 121 miles or 195 kilometrs daily, they leave behind piles of poop. The droppings not only contain food for animals like dung beetles, but also seeds of trees and other plants. As elephants spread new growth far and wide, they are considered a "keystone species," meaning they are important to the life of plants and animals.

Sleeping On Your Toes

Elephant's feet look flat, but the skeleton inside shows a heel that is higher than the toes. The toes are cushioned by big pads. These pads help support the enormous weight and also explain why elephants move about so quietly. At night, wild elephants sleep for as little as two hours, mostly on their toes. That way they can be alert to any danger.

Tusks For Trinkets? No Way!

An elephant's tusks are both a blessing and a curse. For the elephants they are a necessary tool for survival, but their tusks also put them at risk of being hunted. Ivory is mainly used for making jewelry and statues that are sold in markets around the world. Many countries have banned the sale of ivory. However, many more need to join the ban so that no elephant needs to suffer.

Author's Note

The seeds of this book started with my visit to Daphne's Elephant Orphanage in Nairobi, Kenya. It was there that I came in contact (literally) with a young elephant named Imenti who proceeded to swallow my arm and lead me around. Daphne's team told me that this was a promising sign since Imenti was recovering from a long sickness. Although at the time, I only saw Daphne in the distance, I could sense the love her presence instilled for her little charges.

A highlight for me as a teacher was when my school class decided to adopt Imenti. We received regular reports about his care and progress. It is a testament to Daphne and her team that Imenti and other orphans like him are alive and thriving in the wilds of Africa today.

To date, Daphne's organization has hand raised over 300 elephants. The mobile vet unit has treated thousands more elephants that became injured by snares, poisoned arrows, territorial fights or disease. Probably the greatest testament to the success of Daphne's Orphans' Project is the fact that over 30 babies have been born in the wild to former orphans. Most endearing is how these same former orphans have returned to visit Daphne and their former keepers over the years.

There were many events from Daphne's life that I wasn't able to include in this book. Daphne was known for saving the lives of not just elephants, but numerous other animals as well. Her heart beat for every living creature and she never knew the word "No" when help was needed. She has been featured in several articles and feature films by National Geographic and PBS as well as an IMAX film, *Born To Be Wild*. She was even knighted by Queen Elizabeth II and became known as Dame Daphne Sheldrick.

Sadly, Daphne passed away on April 12, 2018 at the age of 83 after a long sickness. Nicknamed "The Elephant Mother," she remained with the elephants she loved to the end. Her legacy continues with her daughters, Jill and Angela, and her grandchildren. Did the elephants sense the death of their great mother? Angela tells of how the morning after Daphne's passing, all the elephant orphans had lined up single file to go past her. "This is something they had never done before," she said. Her words serve as yet another example of how deeply elephants are able to empathize.

For more information about Daphne, you can visit sheldrickwildlifetrust.org online or read books or articles about her. My personal favorite is *The Unsung Heroes*, in which Daphne pays tribute to the many rangers, keepers, and local tribesmen, and women who have shared the family's love for elephants.

BIBLIOGRAPHY

Calkin, Jessamy. "The Woman Who Fosters Elephants in Kenya." The Telegraph, Telegraph Media Group, 24 February 2012.

Chadwick, Douglas. "35 who made a difference: Daphne Sheldrick." Smithsonian.com, 1 November 2005.

Chu, Simon, director. MyWild Affair: The Elephant Who Found a Mom, Season 1, episode 2, PBS, 14 January 2014.

Clifton, Merrit. "Daphne Sheldrick, 83, Showed Kenya That Wildlife Is Worth Most When Alive, " Animals 24-7, 15 April 2018.

Clifton, Merrit, et. al. "A Matriarch Remembers, by Daphne Sheldrick, D.B.E. (1934-2018)" Animals 24-7, 14 April 2014.

Cressey, Daniel. Q&A: "Elephant rescuer." Nature, volume 476, p. 281. 18 Aug. 2011.

Laffrey, Anna. "Mama elephant': How Daphne Sheldrick changed the fate of elephants worldwide." CNN. 15 August 2018.

Lickley, David, director. Born To Be Wild. IMAX 3D, 2011.

Neme, Laurel. "Elephant Foster Mom. A Conversation with Daphne Sheldrick," National Geographic, 6 December 2013.

Sheldrick, Daphne, and Mia Collis. The Unsung Heroes. Sheldrick Wildlife Trust, 2019.

Sheldrick, Daphne. An African Love Story Love, Life and Elephants. Penguin, 2013.

About the Author

R.G. de Rouen is originally from Carmel, California and has been working for more than 25 years as an elementary teacher in international schools throughout the world. He is a graduate of the Institute For Children's Literature in Connecticut and enjoys teaching creative writing skills to his students.

Watching elephants by the waterhole together with his wife is R.G. de Rouen's favorite memory while on safari in Kenya!

About the Illustrator

Kateryna Rohotova (Kate) is an illustrator from Ukraine. She graduated from Luhansk State Institute of Culture and Arts as a digital artist. She worked for eight years as a 2D artist in the gaming industry, but in 2018 she became a freelance artist. Now her favorite part of her job is creating watercolors illustrations for children's books. Her hobbies include handmade crafts, photography, cooking, and aquariums, but drawing is the main passion of her life.

What Can Kids Do To Help?

-Don't buy anything containing ivory.

-Find out if ivory has been banned in your country. If not, you can write your government and ask them to join the ban on all ivory hunting and trade.

-Adopt an elephant and get updates on the orphan's progress by visiting the Orphans Project in Kenya in person or visit their website for more information: https://www.sheldrickwildlifetrust.org

-Look into other elphant protection programs where you might be able to help. I can also recommend the following organizations: National Geographic, WWF, Save the Elephants, or Tusk to name a few. They each have a nice kids' section.

THANK YOU
so much for purchasing this book!

It is my hope that you enjoyed this truly inspiring life story of Daphne Sheldrick. I would be most grateful if you were to leave a review and help me spread the word. Thank you so much!

As a **BONUS** for your purchase, grab my **FREE** booklet, including an extra scene and fun ice cream in a bag activity!

R.G. de Rouen

Get your FREE extra scene and ice cream activity!

www.rgderouen/icecream